THIS WORKBOOK BELONGS TO:

....

....

....

....

the I Love my life challenge

The Art & Science of Reconnecting with Your Life: A Breakthrough Guide to Spark Joy, Innovation, and Growth

An Interactive 28-Day Workbook for Change

From Bestselling Author

ADAM MARKEL

simple truths
Small books. BIG IMPACT.

Published by Simple Truths, an imprint of Sourcebooks
P.O. Box 4410, Naperville, Illinois 60567-4410
(630) 961-3900
sourcebooks.com

Printed and bound in the United States of America.
VP 10 9 8 7 6 5 4 3 2 1

Contents

Introduction: Welcome to the I Love My Life Challenge   *vii*

Week 1: The Power of Resilience   **1**

Day 1   2

Day 2   4

Day 3   6

Day 4   8

Day 5   10

Day 6   12

Day 7   14

Weekly Reflection   16

Week 2: Recover Yourself   **21**

Day 8   24

Day 9   26

Day 10   28

Day 11   30

Day 12   32

Day 13   34

Day 14   36

Weekly Reflection   38

Week 3: Come into Your Own   **43**

Day 15   44

Day 16   46

Day 17   48

Day 18   50

Day 19   52

Day 20   54

Day 21   56

Weekly Reflection   58

Week 4: Grace   **63**

Day 22   64

Day 23   66

Day 24   68

Day 25   70

Day 26   72

Day 27   74

Day 28   76

Weekly Reflection   78

Challenge Wrap-Up: Creating a Life You Love   *83*

Acknowledgments   *84*

About the Author   *85*

Welcome to the I Love My Life Challenge

For many CEOs, professionals, and individuals, the inability to respond to unexpected change can have dire consequences ranging from despair to even suicide. Resilience provides an anchor through the storms of rapid change. It gives us the resolve to not just survive, but thrive in challenging circumstances.

As a resiliency expert, speaker, and author, I discovered a set of simple, yet powerful questions that transformed my life and my clients' lives. It begins with: What if you decided to love your life, no matter what? This is why I created *The I Love My Life Challenge: How to Love Life, in ALL Circumstances, and Create Little Moments for Big Growth.*

I know the devastation of burnout and the consequences of ignoring the shifting sands of the workplace. Twice I found myself at a dead end in my career that I hadn't seen coming, despite what I now can identify as the obvious warning signs. I brought myself back to life with this challenge. And now, as I and so many face change once again, it is no different. In fact, the global pandemic that has sidelined so many and shifted the sands beneath all of our feet is the perfect example of when this challenge is most required and useful. If you can apply these small but powerful practices in the midst of the storm, you **become** the eye of that storm. And your calm becomes your greatest asset and ally. By unapologetically loving my life, no matter what, I raised myself to a new level of awareness, personal fulfillment, and success.

When you love your life regardless of circumstances, you become a resilient leader. You are able to recharge, innovate, and anticipate change faster than ever (because you aren't afraid of it to begin with). You stay on the growth edge, able to sail with the winds of change rather than against them. In this age of technology, the rapid pace of change is causing extreme stress, anxiety, and even increased cases of suicide. Loving your life restores you physically, emotionally, mentally, and even spiritually. It enables you to anticipate change and innovate for the future.

Here's my vision for you: By taking on this challenge, you will discover your inner compass to self-recovery, self-guidance, and even self-love. You will become more relevant and agile in the marketplace. Your business will catapult to higher levels of success. You will regain your sense of mastery and awe. You will *live* in grace.

And grace is something all of us need right now. With the constant shift of politics, pandemics, and global markets, we live in a time of unprecedented change. How have you, personally, been impacted by unexpected change in the past year? Has the change made it hard for you to fully love your life right now?

Like many, you may have experienced massive upheaval—market disruption, business failure, job loss, divorce, or death of a loved one. Or maybe you're dealing with small but persistent change—technology, rules, expectations, to name a few. The relentless pace of change can be overwhelming. How can you be happy in the face of...uh, *everything*?

MAYBE YOU ARE:

- ▸ a burned-out CEO or leader who has lost vision and direction
- ▸ an overwhelmed professional who must reinvent to stay relevant
- ▸ in your thirties, but you already feel obsolete with the latest technology
- ▸ an individual who just feels irrelevant and alone
- ▸ someone who simply feels they do not belong

MAYBE YOU ARE:

- ▸ working for someone you don't like, in a place you don't like
- ▸ caught up in achieving and striving, but you have no joy
- ▸ completely at a loss for where to turn and where to start

AND MAYBE YOU FEEL:

- ▶ exhausted, burned out, depleted
- ▶ fearful, doubtful, or worried
- ▶ overwhelmed by the pace of change
- ▶ disappointed, depressed, or even suicidal
- ▶ resigned and cynical

The sense of failure and lack of connection can erode our performance, exuberance, and love for life.

With all the societal shifts going on, life seems to be changing faster than ever. Maybe you have a feeling that you too should change direction, but you don't know how. And you can't trust yourself to do it.

As a leader—of a business, profession, or your life—your biggest risk is unexpected change. And the biggest challenge is whether you will face it by choice or default.

Living by choice keeps you agile, relevant, and alive. It makes you resilient.
Living by default can lead to dissatisfaction and doubt.

With all the changes going on around us, sometimes the hardest thing to change is our own minds. But beliefs can be changed in a matter of seconds. And a life can be restored in a matter of hours and days.

This is your guide.

This interactive journal will break down all the internal barriers you are clinging to and help you learn how to love your life, regardless of circumstances. Because there will ALWAYS be circumstances, so we need to learn how to overcome, to become resilient, and to love our lives anyway.

Join me on this four-week, twenty-eight-day challenge and start to love your life again—fully, and without strings attached (or qualifications or prerequisites).

Let's begin.

Scan me with a camera phone for more content!

When we are no longer able to change a situation, we are challenged to change ourselves.

—VIKTOR FRANKL

The Power of Resilience

As I witnessed the floundering of my own CEO career, I questioned everything, including my convictions that had previously brought success. I asked myself, *What if I love my life, no matter what?* It transformed my beliefs about what was possible in life.

Changing our beliefs can be one of the hardest things to do. Our beliefs give us comfort, an anchor in rough seas. But beliefs that worked during one period of our lives often don't serve us well in another stage of life. I couldn't continue to "guard" everything in my life the way I learned as a nineteen-year-old lifeguard on the beach.

Holding on to that mindset hurt my career and almost cut short my life.

For others, their beliefs lead them to isolation and even despair. We see it in our falling life expectancy and in the rash of suicides among successful entrepreneurs. With a willingness to love your life and embrace change, you can develop the resilience you need to thrive. Are you ready to go to the next level of excellence? If you commit to love your life, no matter what, new possibilities will open up for you.

What commitments are you ready to make today, right now, to yourself, to fully begin to love your life?

I commit to...

....

....

....

SIGNATURE: .... DATE: ....

There are only two options regarding commitment. You're either
in or out. There's no such thing as a life in between.
—PAT RILEY

Day 1

In the *I Love My Life Challenge*—loving your life no matter what—the real challenge is letting go of beliefs that no longer serve us.

I want you to let go of these old ideas and mantras before you become as miserable as I was. You shouldn't have to hit bottom to know you're off course. Identifying and letting go of outdated beliefs gives you the space to embrace new ones. Your new beliefs allow you to live by choice, instead of default. They give you vision, resilience, and the harvest.

Which beliefs are holding you back? Which can drive you forward? Identify and map your opportunities in the lines and diagram that follow.

Beliefs that once worked but are now holding me back

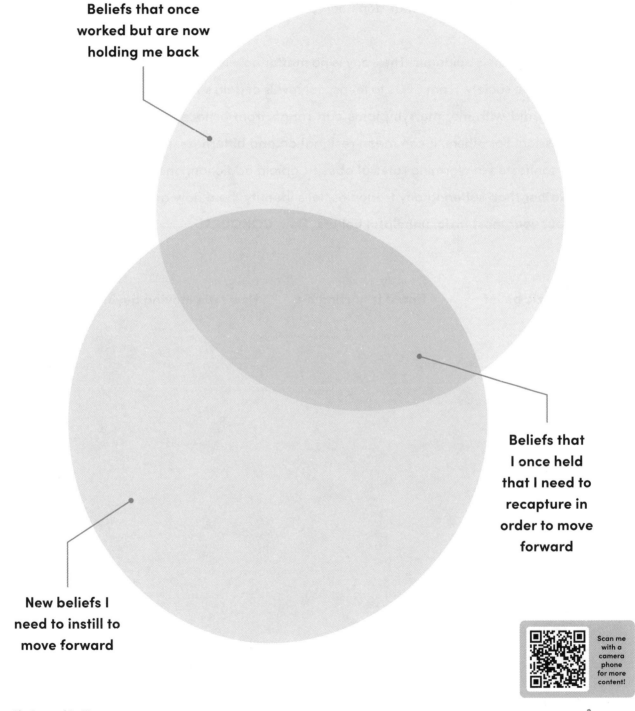

Beliefs that I once held that I need to recapture in order to move forward

New beliefs I need to instill to move forward

Scan me with a camera phone for more content!

Day 2

At the worst level, beliefs that don't serve us can lead to despair, isolation, and deep depression.

Our despair is epidemic. The irony is no matter how isolated we feel, we are suffering as an entire society. From CEOs to teens, our levels of pain sound an urgent wake-up call.

As it did with me, the symptoms can range from exhaustion to hopelessness and depression. For others, it can mean resignation and bitterness. In the United States, this has manifested in alarming rates of obesity, opioid addiction, and suicide.

Rather than suffering any tragedies, let's identify them now and push beyond them. **List out your most toxic, unhelpful beliefs.** Then **CONQUER!**

Toxic belief	How it is hurting me	How I am moving beyond this belief

> What you think upon grows. Whatever you allow
> to occupy your mind you magnify in your life.
>
> —EMMET FOX

Toxic belief	How it is hurting me	How I am moving beyond this belief

Scan me with a camera phone for more content!

Day 3

As a society, we're taught to "Live to fight another day." It's time to change that. Instead, we can "Live to *love* another day."

When we love our lives regardless of circumstance, we become resilient leaders. We are able to recharge, innovate, and anticipate change faster than ever. We stay on the growth edge, able to sail with the winds of change rather than against them. When we lead with love, we serve as role models to others. We can reset our minds, emotions, bodies, and spirits to restore ourselves and become masters of our lives. We can lead our businesses and teams to create cultures of loving resilience.

So, let's share the love. Fill up the hearts below. What do we love, right now, about our jobs, lives, selves, or opportunities? Find the silver linings and let's make them *shine*.

I'm thankful for my struggle because without it,
I wouldn't have stumbled across my strength.
—ALEXANDRA ELLE

Scan me with a camera phone for more content!

Day 4

Change itself is not bad. In the history of life on earth, it's not the biggest or strongest who survive. It's the ones who can adapt most quickly, the ones who stay relevant over time. As a human species, we've always faced change. We've always found a way to overcome obstacles and emerge stronger. That's resilience.

Resilience draws on the inner strength we all have and provides an anchor through the storms of rapid change. It gives us the grit to not just survive but thrive in challenging circumstances.

As a former lifeguard, I know that best practice is to stock a boat with life jackets before setting sail. In the same way, resilience is something you create before you need it. It means planning for disruption before it happens, reinventing before you get the ax, and innovating before you become irrelevant. By cultivating resilience, you make yourself neutral to change.

Let's plan for the worst. **What are your safety plans, your lifeguard attitude (or disposition or conviction or philosophy), that you need to apply to your mindset to feel secure as you venture out in your new goals?**

> Think twice before you speak, because your words and influence will
> plant the seed of either success or failure in the mind of another.
> —NAPOLEON HILL

Scan me with a camera phone for more content!

Day 5

Rescuing yourself from despair, from hardships brought on by rapid change, is a personal journey, but you're not alone. As an individual, you have your loved ones—family and friends—willing to listen, support, and build you up. Ready to lend a hand. Professionally, you're part of our community of clients and individuals who have taken on difficult change themselves, many with incredible results. Find those mentors in your network who have overcome and ask them how. Even if you are no longer actively employed or tied to a specific company, find that community and learn how to grow as these leaders have. **Using the tools below, identify your supporters!**

Issue	Support or Mentor	How they can help me and what I hope to share

> Be a rock to others in need...but also, be a rock who recognizes that you
> also will experience times when you need to seek your own rock.
>
> —BYRON PULSIFER

Issue	Support or Mentor	How they can help me and what I hope to share

Scan me with a camera phone for more content!

Day 6

Yesterday and the day before, we identified a collection of issues you're creating safety plans for, along with individuals you believe can help you overcome. Now, it is time to tap those resources.

Below are two letter templates. **Write to two of the individuals you identified and sketch out how you'd like their support.** This can be the script you use when chatting with them over your upcoming needs, the email you send asking for support, or even the letter you have hand delivered to their door!

DEAR ....**,**

....

....

....

....

....

....

....

....

....

....

....

SIGNED, ...

....

Sometimes asking for help is the bravest move
you can make. You don't have to go it alone.
—ANONYMOUS

DEAR _____,

_____

_____

_____

_____

_____

_____

_____

_____

_____

_____

_____

_____

_____

_____

_____

_____

SIGNED, _____

_____

Day 7

Becoming resilient in times of great change is a challenge not because of the actual hardships but because of our own reactions. Now that you have outlined all the things holding you back, let's focus on all the things building you up! What are you doing right? What makes you an awesome person, friend, leader, member of society, *change maker*?

I love ....

I can use this ....

....

I love ....

I can use this ....

....

I love ....

I can use this ....

....

I love ....

I can use this ....

....

I love ....

I can use this ....

....

> *What we have once enjoyed we can never lose...*
> *All that we love deeply becomes a part of us.*
> —HELEN KELLER

I love
_____

I can use this
_____

_____

I love
_____

I can use this
_____

_____

I love
_____

I can use this
_____

_____

I love
_____

I can use this
_____

_____

I love
_____

I can use this
_____

_____

I love
_____

I can use this
_____

_____

Weekly Reflection

As week 1 comes to a close, hopefully you have identified all the toxic and limiting beliefs and built up a path toward resilience for yourself. **What has impacted your thinking most this week? What will you need to bring forward and improve upon going forward to truly let go and grow?**

....

....

....

....

....

....

....

....

....

....

....

....

....

....

....

....

....

....

Self-care is never a selfish act—it is simply good stewardship of
the only gift I have, the gift I was put on earth to offer to others.
—PARKER PALMER

Self-care is giving the world the best of you, instead of what's left of you.

—KATIE REED

These fantasies about the future, based on the past, are the hope and hype we con ourselves with. Even if we get what we always wanted, it never looks like we thought it would when it arrives.

—BRAD BLANTON

Recover Yourself

One of the hardest things about times of great change that overwhelm and burn us out is the feeling we get where we have lost ourselves. Looking at your life, wondering how you got to where you are...that dim feeling of confusion paired with multiple failures as you recognize how off track you are from your goals.

This week, we are going to focus on how to bring forward the best in ourselves in order to once again become someone we recognize. We made great headway on day 7 last week (page 14) by outlining some of the things we love about ourselves. Now let's do some deeper exploration...

What goals do you have for yourself that you don't see or even identify with the person you are now? **List out as many goals, traits, and dreams you would like to see actualized as you can in the squares below!** Some examples might be small and personal, such as read more or make your child feel special each day. Others might be professional, such as get a new contact this month or clear your inbox at the end of each week. Some should be big—professional or personal—like land a new client or learn a new language. What would you like your life to look like?

For Example:

1. I LOVE MY...

2.

3.

Happiness is letting go of what you think your life is supposed
to look like and celebrating it for everything that it is.
—MANDY HALE

13.

14.

12.

16.

17.

15.

20.

18.

19.

Day 8

Radical Honesty is about facing the truth of what's not working. It's about moving from fear and denial to making more conscious choices and decisions. In business, it means telling the truth about your market, your industry, your company, and your job. It means clearly facing business challenges, anticipating future trends, and finding ways to innovate—before someone or something else forces you to change. In life, it's about inviting feedback and then consciously choosing to change.

Radical Honesty ultimately frees you. In our week 2 kickoff, we identified where we want to be, how we want to grow, and goals we have in mind. Now, it's time to get real with ourselves about where we are. **Being as realistic as possible, repeat your grid, but instead of re-identifying your hopes, let's identify why they are not your reality. What's the hold up?**

1.

2.

3.

4.

5.

If you want to be happy, set a goal that commands your thoughts,
liberates your energy, and inspires your hopes.
—ANDREW CARNEGIE

7.

8.

6.

10.

11.

9.

14.

12.

13.

Day 9

Whew, we did not pull any punches with day 8! Identifying what has been holding us back is unfortunately the only way we can move forward. Thankfully, we humans are not geared toward failure. Where you are now doesn't have to be where your story ends.

Today, let's take this (now familiar) grid and **write out our next steps to success.** In each square, I want you to put down your first baby step to achievement. Refer back to what this goal, trait, or hope is and then why it isn't a reality. Perhaps the goal is to be a positive force on your team. What's the easiest, most actionable, first step you can think of? "Start every team meeting with a joke"? "Ask my teammate how they are before every conversation"? **Using your goals and then what you have identified as lacking, find the missing links.**

1.

2.

3.

5.

4.

It's the little details that are vital. Little things make big things happen.

—JOHN WOODEN

6.

7.

8.

9.

10.

11.

12.

13.

14.

Day 10

Looking at your three radically honest grids: Do you notice any themes? Do many of your goals rely on you pushing yourself to be more positive? To finding more time in the week?

There is likely an overall weakness that is holding you back across multiple goals. Knowing this about yourself, **how can you use your strongest traits to overcome?**

You are strong when you know your weakness. You are beautiful when you appreciate your flaws. You are wise when you learn from your mistakes.

—UNKNOWN

Scan me with a camera phone for more content!

Day 11

We've gotten radically honest about ourselves. It's time to REFRAME all the external circumstances that are constantly being thrown at us. As an example, CEOs constantly face crisis. On a professional or personal level, we meet challenges and setbacks daily. Yet, as a leader, you can change crises to opportunity just by reframing the situation. This means seeing challenges differently. It means changing your perspective, without changing the circumstances. Reframing allows you to detach from a challenge so you can find the opportunity for growth.

Instead of reacting to a crisis, resilient leaders ask, "What's the creative opportunity here?" And then they take action. In your business and life, take an inventory of the outside obstacles and reframe each one. **Where are the creative opportunities?**

Obstacle	Opportunity

> You must learn a new way to think before you can master a new way to be.
> —MARIANNE WILLIAMSON

Obstacle	Opportunity

Scan me with a camera phone for more content!

Day 12

Taking your BIGGEST and most EXCITING opportunity from day 11, let's get into the nitty-gritty. **Map out your action plan and initial goals.**

Action Plan

Step 1: ....

....

....

....

....

....

....

....

....

....

....

....

....

....

....

You don't have to be great to start, but you do have to start to be great.

—ZIG ZIGLAR

Initial Goals

Step 1:

Day 13

Often when we are looking at the discrepancy between our goals and where we find ourselves, it is time to reenvision our next steps and go back to basics. In business and life, we can become so overwhelmed in the experiences of living that we lose the lessons. To regain the meaning in our lives, we need to create a powerful new vision. This entails mining insights from our past to take us into the future.

When we deliberately look for insights in our lives, consciously finding the wisdom in our experiences, we can let go of past challenges. We are no longer at the mercy of the winds, waters, and weather of life. The new vision we create charts a new course for the future. We are tacking into the wind, creating intentional progress and direction. You've mapped out your goals, your limits, and your biggest opportunities. With all of this in mind, let's pause to reflect on the next steps. **Where is your overall vision leading you?** If your heart isn't aligning on certain tasks, let's go back and revise.

> You perform better in every area of your life when your thoughts, feelings, emotions, goals, and values are in alignment.
> —BRIAN TRACY

Scan me with a camera phone for more content!

Day 14

It's time to recharge and fully recover yourself as week 2 draws to a close. When I say "recharge," I mean fully renew yourself, by any means necessary. It's a way to return to our natural rhythms so we can refuel the tank and rehab the motor. Recharge happens at all levels: physical, mental, emotional, and even spiritual. The goal is to renew, refresh, and regenerate, spawning fresh ideas and capacity for more. Whether on a business, career, or personal level, recharging strengthens us as teams and individuals.

The best way to recharge your business and life on a daily basis is through rituals. One way to help you determine which rituals to establish is to understand your starting point: In which areas of resilience do you require the most recharge? Find out by scanning the QR code below to take our resilience assessment.

Understanding your baseline, what areas of resilience require the most recharge? What rituals can you rely on in times of stress? How can you make time for them daily, weekly, monthly, or simply as needed?

Ritual:

Benefit:

Where does this fit in my routine?

When you recover or discover something that nourishes your soul and brings joy, care enough about yourself to make room for it in your life.
—JEAN SHINODA BOLEN

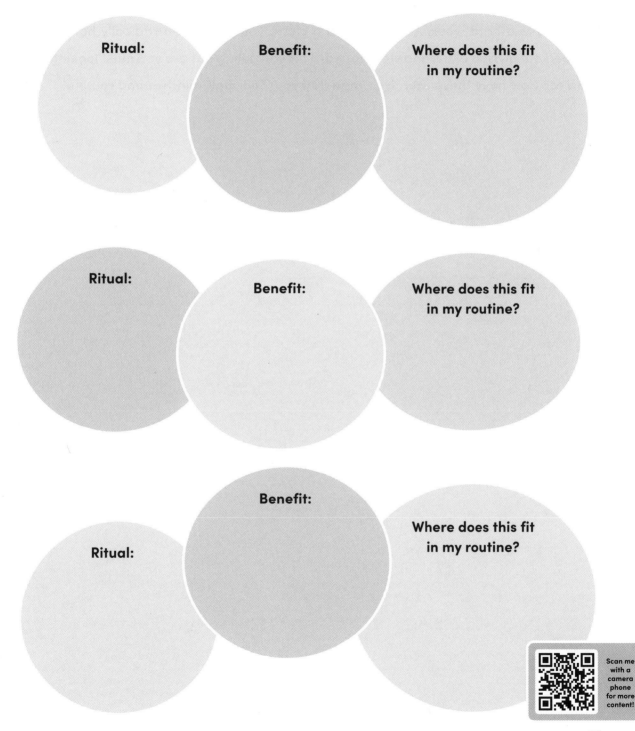

Ritual:

Benefit:

Where does this fit in my routine?

Ritual:

Benefit:

Where does this fit in my routine?

Benefit:

Ritual:

Where does this fit in my routine?

Scan me with a camera phone for more content!

Weekly Reflection

DATE: /   /

This week is a hard week. As it comes to a close, you have been radically honest and mapped out myriad plans and steps forward for yourself. **What are you most looking forward to? How have these exercises impacted your "normal" mindset and routine?**

Looking forward to things is half the pleasure of them. You mayn't get the things themselves; but nothing can prevent you from having the fun of looking forward to them.

—ANNE, *ANNE OF GREEN GABLES* BY L. M. MONTGOMERY

Scan me with a camera phone for more content!

A wise man will make more opportunities than he finds.

—FRANCIS BACON

The very essence of leadership is that you have to have a vision. It's got to be a vision you articulate clearly and forcefully on every occasion. You can't blow an uncertain trumpet.

—THEODORE HESBURGH

Come into Your Own

We are all leaders. But moving beyond basic leadership means coming into your own. For business leaders, this may mean rebooting your corporate position, relaunching your existing business, or starting a new one. As a resilient leader, you lead with purpose. You easily enroll and onboard others. You distill your existing skills, knowledge, and experiences, refining them in your next level of growth. With your team, you do what it takes to reach the next goal.

So what is your next goal? I've had you map everything from small goals to big limits. Where do you want to lead your team? What's first?

....

....

....

....

....

....

....

....

....

....

....

....

....

....

Scan me with a camera phone for more content!

Day 15

Resilient leaders are able to improvise—to create, innovate, and open up possibilities for the future. One way to achieve this is through mentorship, learning from others who have walked this path. Another way is through coaching, where powerful questions open new possibilities for the future. As you take forward all these new skills and visions we've been working on in the first two weeks, who can you bring with you? Look at your professional goals and identify some opportunities to bring your team forward, to bring your company success, and even to mentor some of the brightest within your network. **List out as many mentorship roles and professional opportunities that you can dream up. How can you move the needle in your career, your profession, and make the world better for it?**

OPPORTUNITY TO LEAD:

> If your actions create a legacy that inspires others to dream more, learn more, do more, and become more, then you are an excellent leader.
> —DOLLY PARTON

OPPORTUNITY TO LEAD:

Day 16

Repeat the same thought experiment from day 15, but this time, apply it to your personal life. What can you do to lead your family, community, or friends forward? Is there something that will make your home environment happier? Make your community better?

You're an *empowering, resilient* leader. List all the ways you can share that in the other aspects of your life.

OPPORTUNITY TO LEAD:

Leadership is not a position or a title, it is action and example.

—DONALD McGANNON

OPPORTUNITY
TO LEAD:

Day 17

Practical mentors teach you useful skills, while others share best practices for career, relationships, or spirituality. Top coaches ask questions and provide exercises to think about problems differently and innovate new solutions. Now that you've listed out all these opportunities to lead and create impact, think about who leads and impacts you. Identify one of your mentors (perhaps refer back to your letter on day 6!) and tie them to one of your projects.

Outline your goals below and how they specifically can support and coach you through them. Create a system for accountability and to regularly check in.

A mentor is someone who sees more talent and ability within you,
than you see in yourself, and helps bring it out of you.

—BOB PROCTOR

Day 18

If you haven't already identified personal and professional mentors from the exercises on days 15 and 16, it's time to do so now. In the last exercise, you outlined and gave real thought as to how one of your mentors or coaches could hold you accountable and lead you to success. Think of those in your life who need support, care, or accountability to achieve some of their big dreams. **How can YOU be the change in their life? Outline a person you can coach, their goal, and your role in making it a reality. Then help them make it happen!**

Great opportunities to help others seldom come, but small ones surround us every day.

—SALLY KOCH

Scan me with a camera phone for more content!

Day 19

At the highest level, leadership, goal achievement, even improvisation starts with an internal knowing that leads to inspired answers. One way to do this is listening to your Highest Guide, maybe through meditation, prayer, or being in nature. (My form of meditation is surfing.)

Take a moment to identify who your Highest Guide is and outline ways to make your "checkpoints" with your greatest "coach."

Who is my Highest Guide? How do I benefit from this connection?

> Nothing glows brighter than the heart awakened
> to the unseen light of love that lives within it.
> —GUY FINLEY

How can I create more time with my Highest Guide in my routine?

Scan me
with a
camera
phone
for more
content!

Day 20

The trim tabs (a.k.a. "small rudders") of a ship allow it to make small turns that can eventually change the entire direction of the vessel. In our businesses and lives, when we make small turns or micro changes, we have the capacity to anticipate change before it's too late to turn. This is agility.

We've mapped out a lot of paths for you to find ways back into love with your life. **Pick one and outline some of the possible pitfalls that, based on your experience, you will have to be ready to address as you pursue.**

The man who moves a mountain begins by carrying away small stones.

—CONFUCIUS

Scan me with a camera phone for more content!

Day 21

As we learned yesterday, the core tenet of agility is planning for change in advance and having the flexibility to innovate before the world, or specific market, forces us to. This includes planning for the worst by creating plan B's, backup teams, and backup systems. In business, it also means planning for internet hacks, electricity failures, and technology changes. It's the difference between proactivity and reactivity.

It's the idea of stocking the ship before setting sail so you have alternative generators and lifeboats. Agility is about moving from living in reaction, which comes from a place of fear, scarcity, and panic, to living in response, which means acting from knowingness, rehearsals, practice, and plans.

What fears can we eliminate (thereby making your life happier) by simply moving forward with agility? How can you tie your fears to agile responses to create overall harmony in your day-to-day?

Fear	Agile Response

> Success today requires the agility and drive to
> constantly rethink, reinvigorate, react, and reinvent.
>
> —BILL GATES

Fear	Agile Response

Scan me with a camera phone for more content!

Weekly Reflection

This week, you should have found your footing as a leader, taking on aspects of mentorship, planning, and agility that you didn't have before. **Do you feel empowered? How do you still feel you need to grow?**

....

....

....

....

....

....

....

....

....

....

....

....

....

....

....

....

....

....

....

You are what you repeatedly do. Excellence is not a singular act but a habit.

—ARISTOTLE

If we're growing, we're always going to be out of our comfort zone.

—JOHN MAXWELL

If you took one-tenth the energy you put into complaining and applied it to solving the problem, you'd be surprised by how well things can work out... Complaining does not work as a strategy. We all have finite time and energy. Any time we spend whining is unlikely to help us achieve our goals. And it won't make us happier.

—RANDY PAUSCH

Grace

Since going on this journey, hopefully you have begun experiencing more harmony, freedom, and abundance. You are growing as a resilient leader. You are creating patterns for joy in your life and opportunities for happiness and achievement that you can lean into.

Change never ends, much like winds never cease. The question is, will you love your life no matter how the winds blow? When you learn to love your life, you experience *grace*, and life will love you back in many unexpected ways. You live an impactful life, with no one left behind.

With all you have learned, how are you bringing your life, community, and overall impact forward?

Scan me with a camera phone for more content!

Day 22

In order to thrive, not just survive, you're going to need to schedule your energy—every day. We've mapped out a lot of paths forward, but those, too, will drain you if you aren't also finding harmony (sometimes called "balance") in your day-to-day. So for true success, your *biggest win* will be if you can find more energy. Most of us are in a state of constant motion; we can't help but GO GO GO! We are all living in a time of tremendous change, and we are seemingly planning to accomplish or die trying...but is that tenable?

List as many activities as you can that give you energy. Closing a deal at work, having a deep conversation with your spouse, making a new professional contact, going for a run in the park, working on a proposal, making a great meal, quiet time with a good book... What fills you with energy that you can then apply to your life to create momentum versus other activities that are either neutral or drain you of energy?

It takes as much energy to wish as it does to plan.

—ELEANOR ROOSEVELT

Scan me with a camera phone for more content!

Day 23

Now that we know what energizes you, let's focus on what drains you. For every activity that gives you energy, there are ten more that drain you. We're going to need to avoid those to have time to maintain this challenge.

So now let's list as many activities as you can that drain your energy. Answering emails, making calls, reviewing your finances, attending status meetings, paying bills... What drains you of energy and grinds your schedule, your plans, and your momentum to a halt?

....

....

....

....

....

....

....

....

....

....

....

....

....

....

....

....

> *I will greet this day with love in my heart.*
>
> —OG MANDINO

Scan me with a camera phone for more content!

Day 24

Now that you know what energizes you, let's take a look at your schedule. What's draining? What energizes you? This isn't about finding time on your calendar; not only does no one have time in their day, but even if you did, time isn't the issue. This is about finding ENERGY. **Create more opportunities for energizing moments and cut those that drain you as much as possible.**

Note, many of the things that drain you are likely to be necessary things in your life, such as paying bills. While you can't simply eliminate that drain, can you simplify it and make it take significantly less of your time? Sure you can: shift to automatic bill pay. Schedule a quarterly check where you ensure all your statements line up and nothing looks like fraud, and take this monthly drain off the schedule. For many, many drains in our lives, there are likely apps, teammates, loved ones, or services we can outsource some or all of the drain. See what needs to live with you and work to trim the rest.

Activity	Does this drain or energize me?	How can I adjust my time accordingly to support more/less of this activity?

These mountains that you are carrying, you were only supposed to climb.

—NAJWA ZEBIAN

Activity	Does this drain or energize me?	How can I adjust my time accordingly to support more/less of this activity?

Day 25

How can we protect our goals, our loved ones, and our lifestyle in these uncertain days without burning out?

The answer is by taking active steps to help us find our callings while avoiding (or addressing) needs and crises. Reading a good book may give us energy, but that can't be the only thing we do with our time, or there won't be any forward momentum. **Looking closely at your schedule once again, adjust here to ensure you are taking energy to apply against your goals and thinking with agility to apply energy to creative crisis management.**

Activity	Does this drain or energize me?	How can I adjust my time accordingly to support more/less of this activity?

> Every morning you have two choices: continue to sleep
> with your dreams, or wake up and chase them.
> —CARMELO ANTHONY

Activity	Does this drain or energize me?	How can I adjust my time accordingly to support more/less of this activity?

Scan me with a camera phone for more content!

Day 26

Now that you've got your energy planned for, let's focus on the other big component in being able to love your life: maintenance. **How are you going to maintain momentum on your goals?**

Movement creates more movement. Movement creates energy. Movement creates life!

—MICHAEL D'AULERIO

Day 27

One of the simplest tactics I have found to remind myself daily of how much I love my life is to literally wake up and exclaim it to myself. (More on that in the challenge wrap-up.) Let's now take some time to create a mantra for you. Something you can go back to and say, daily, that is in alignment with your BIG GOALS for happiness. I call this the 10-Second Reset!

You have a few big goals mapped out. Now come up with mantras to match! Write as many as you can think of, and then pick the most empowering for yourself out of the batch.

> The words you speak become the house you live in.
>
> —HAFIZ

Day 28

This challenge is no small feat, and here you are! On the final day! By now, you will have learned how to become more resilient, how to identify and overcome your challenges and limitations, how to empower yourself and lead others, how to plan for change, how to find energy, and generally how to THRIVE and live every day with a life you love!

The last thing I can offer you is that happiness begins and ends with you. I've guided you and you've created road maps for success, backup plans to ensure you achieve your goals, mantras to refocus your mindset, and maintenance plans for your energy. Hopefully all these components will help you to find happiness and success! However, your attitude is yours alone. Only *you* can start the day deciding to be happier and not just going through the motions of these plans. Only *you* can live these plans to their fullest potential. And only *you* can answer how exactly happiness will work in your own life, day by day, minute by minute.

So. How can you find happiness, find optimism, every day? Where can you bring positivity into your mindset, and how can you make it last?

Waiting for someone else to make you happy is the best way to be sad.

—UNKNOWN

Scan me with a camera phone for more content!

Weekly Reflection

YOU DID IT! We'll celebrate further in the wrap-up next, but knowing what you know now... what if, no matter what, we determined we were going to love our lives? **How is this mind-set going to change everything about your life, starting now?**

Once your mindset changes, everything on the outside will change along with it.

—STEVE MARABOLI

> **Nothing is impossible. The word itself says "I'm Possible."**
>
> —AUDREY HEPBURN

Scan me with a camera phone for more content!

As James Taylor sings, "The secret of life is enjoying the passage of time. Try not to try too hard; it's just a lovely ride."

Creating a Life You Love

I've always been inspired by movies and believe that great movies can be a great inspiration in our lives, and the film I'm about to mention was certainly an inspirational moment for me.

Many years ago, I was watching *Jerry Maguire*, and I felt so inspired by the character of Jerry's mentor, Dicky Fox, a quirky and sweet old-school salesman who shared his philosophy of business and life...and how he loved his wife and he loved his life!

It was intriguing to me, and before I knew it, I repeated his words out loud: **"I love my life."**

I remember thinking how good it felt to make that declaration, so I repeated it again: "I love my life!"

Before long, it had turned into a daily mantra, a prayer, and a VERY powerful intention that began to change my experience of living and being. You now have all the tools at your disposal to create a life you love, every single day. And more importantly, craft a life that will love you right back.

Are you ready to shout? Yell it now, loud and proud: **I LOVE MY LIFE!**

Scan me with a camera phone for more content!

Acknowledgments

My family has been my greatest support. My wife, Randi, has been my rock. I am eternally grateful to be alive to see the epic changes and opportunities for growth in the world. My heart is filled with appreciation for my partners, Randi, Deanna, and Chelsea; to Sourcebooks; and to my editor, Meg Gibbons, for their great efforts in bringing this vision to fruition.

About the Author

Adam Markel is a #1 *Wall Street Journal, USA Today, Los Angeles Times,* and *Publishers Weekly* bestselling author of *Pivot: The Art and Science of Reinventing Your Career and Life* and *Soul Over Matter: Ancient and Modern Wisdom and Practical Techniques to Create Unlimited Abundance.*

As a sought-after keynote speaker and workshop facilitator, Adam reaches tens of thousands of audience members worldwide each year with his message of resilience. His viral TEDx Talk has inspired and guided hundreds of thousands of people to start their day with love. His book *The I Love My Life Challenge* offers a lifeboat to business and general-interest readers seeking to stay dynamic, engaged, and relevant in their careers and lives in the face of unprecedented change.

What Adam discovered personally—and through working with tens of thousands of people and businesses facing the challenges of rapid change—is that choosing to love and be grateful for one's life is critical to staying resilient in business and life.

These include the burned-out CEO who feels the inner urge to make big changes, yet fears losing his or her position; the overwhelmed senior-career professional who must reinvent to stay relevant; the mid-career worker suffering "early life crisis," whose skills are outdated in the face of new technology; the young business graduate who wonders how to navigate a future career as the concepts of traditional jobs continue to shift; and people who simply feel disenfranchised, marginalized, or even suicidal because they don't feel they belong. As leaders of their businesses, careers, and lives, these individuals are losing resilience in the face of change because they no longer feel relevance and belonging.

The cost is high. American CEOs are suffering what BestLife.com calls "the financial post-traumatic stress syndrome," with outcomes ranging from depression to suicide. Suicide rates have jumped alarmingly for

Scan me with a camera phone for more content!

working adults, according to the *Pacific Standard*. According to the *World Happiness Report 2019*, coauthored by bestselling author and economist Jeffrey Sachs, Americans continue to decline in overall happiness. This is because Americans are experiencing less "social support" as the United States turns into a "mass-addiction society."

The I Love My Life Challenge is a guide for businesses and individuals to move from surviving to thriving. Using case studies, current research, and anecdotes from Adam's life and others', *The I Love My Life Challenge* shows that resilience is not just a good idea in business and life, it's imperative—offering a lifeboat to transform our businesses, relationships, and lives.